REVIVAL
IN THE LAND

38 EASY ARRANGEMENTS FOR REVIVAL CHOIR

by Mosie Lister

Lillenas PUBLISHING COMPANY

KANSAS CITY, MO 64141

Contents

I Saw the Light

H. W.

HANK WILLIAMS
Arr. by Mosie Lister

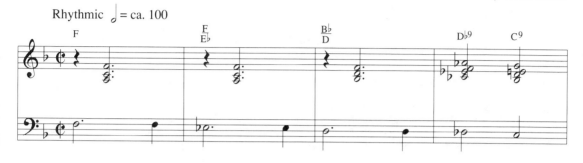

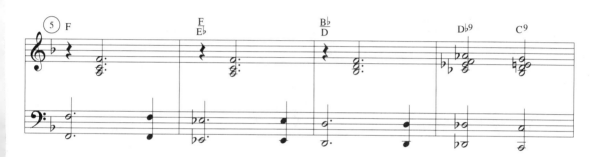

1. I wan-dered so aim-less,
2. Just like a blind man, I

life filled with sin; I would-n't let my
wan-dered a-long; Wor-ries and fears I

8

He Looked Beyond My Fault

DOTTIE RAMBO

Adapted from "Londonderry Aire"
Arr. by Mosie Lister

10

Praise the Lord Medley

I Just Came to Praise the Lord
O Come, Let Us Adore Him

Arr. by David Miller Williams

12

13

We Bring the Sacrifice of Praise

K. D.

KIRK DEARMAN

O for a Thousand Tongues

D. B.

DAVID BINION
Arr. by Mosie Lister

16

Revival in the Land

R. M.

RENEE MORRIS
Arr. by Mosie Lister

19

It's Beginning to Rain

GLORIA GAITHER, A. W.

WILLIAM J. GAITHER,
AARON WILBURN
Arr. by Mosie Lister

23

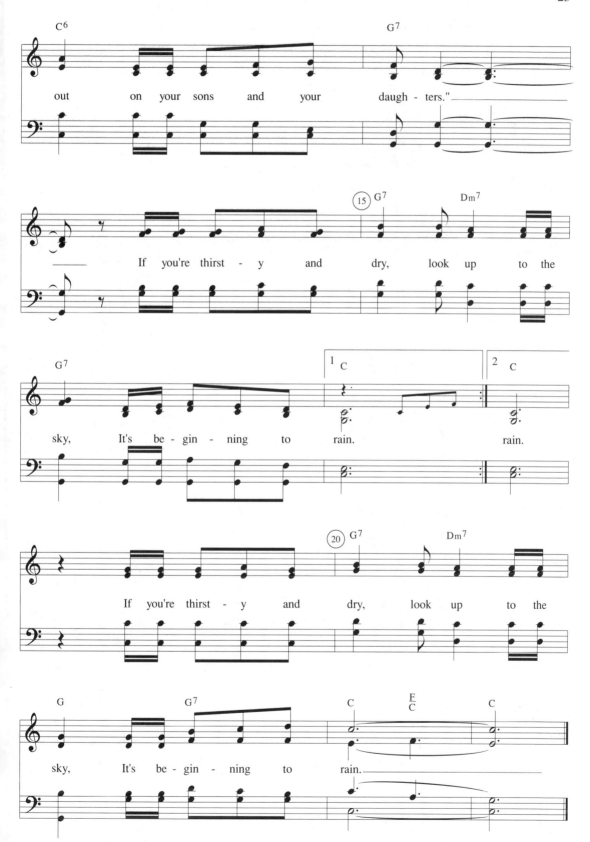

Holy Spirit Medley

Come, Holy Spirit
I Need Thee Every Hour

Arr. by Mosie Lister

* "Come, Holy Spirit" (William J. and Gloria Gaither)

Come, Ho - ly Spir - it, I need Thee;

Come, sweet Spir - it, I pray.

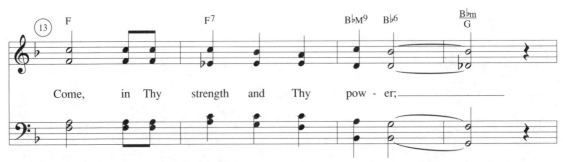

Come, in Thy strength and Thy pow - er;

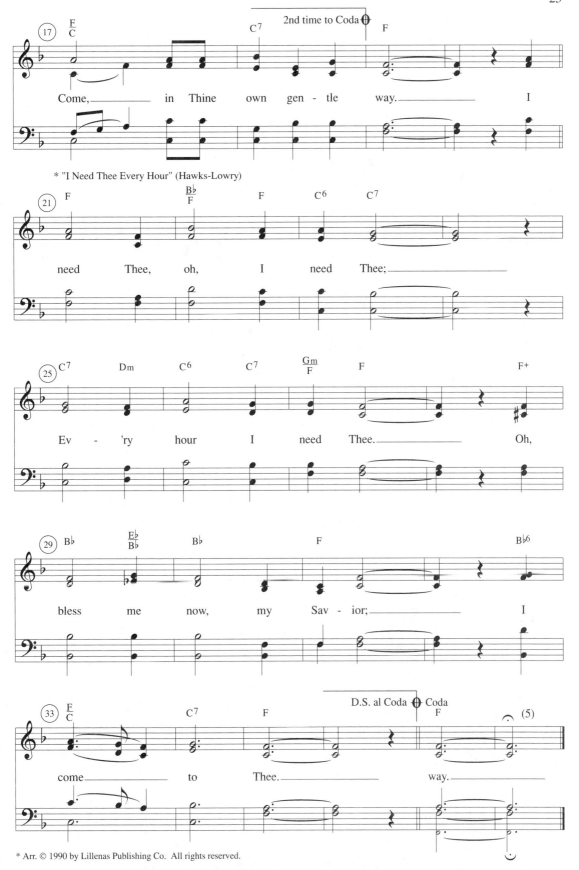

* "I Need Thee Every Hour" (Hawks-Lowry)

Triumphantly the Church Will Rise

K. T.

KIRK TALLEY
Arr. by Mosie Lister

27

'Til the Storm Passes By

M. L.

MOSIE LISTER
*Arr. by Rick Powell
and Mosie Lister*

32

Sing a Simple Song of Faith

DAVID STEELE

MOSIE LISTER

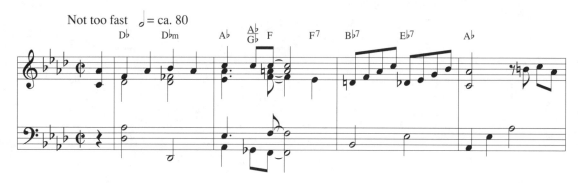

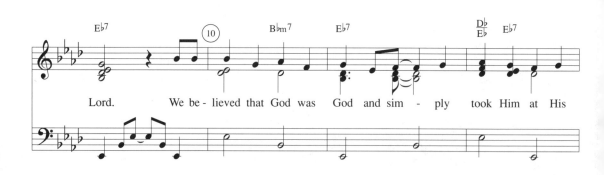

35

He's So Good

M. L.

MOSIE LISTER

With motion ♩. = ca. 84

I__ will praise_____ Him, praise_____

Him, Praise_____ the Lord;_____ He's so good to

me. I__ will me. In the morn-ing,_____ in the mid-night,_____ On

Where No One Stands Alone

*M. L.

MOSIE LISTER

*Inspired by Psalm 27:14; 51:10-12; 55:22

41

Come and Dine

C. B. W.

C. B. WIDMEYER
Arr. by Mosie Lister

44

* Opt. add men unison on melody.

45

46

Listen, Jesus Is Calling You

Traditional

Traditional
Arr. by Mosie Lister and
Lyndell Leatherman

When We Hear the Trumpet Sound

M. L.

MOSIE LISTER

How Long Has It Been?

M. L.

MOSIE LISTER

52

53

Great and Mighty

M. B.

MARLENE BIGLEY

Lyrics:

Great and might-y is the Lord our God,____ Great and might-y is He.____ Great and might-y is the Lord our God,____ Great and might-y is He.

Since I Have Been Redeemed

E. O. E.

EDWIN O. EXCELL
Arr. by Mosie Lister

Then I Met the Master

M. L.

MOSIE LISTER

59

60

I've Been Changed

M. L.

MOSIE LISTER

63

Restore My Soul

M. L.

MOSIE LISTER

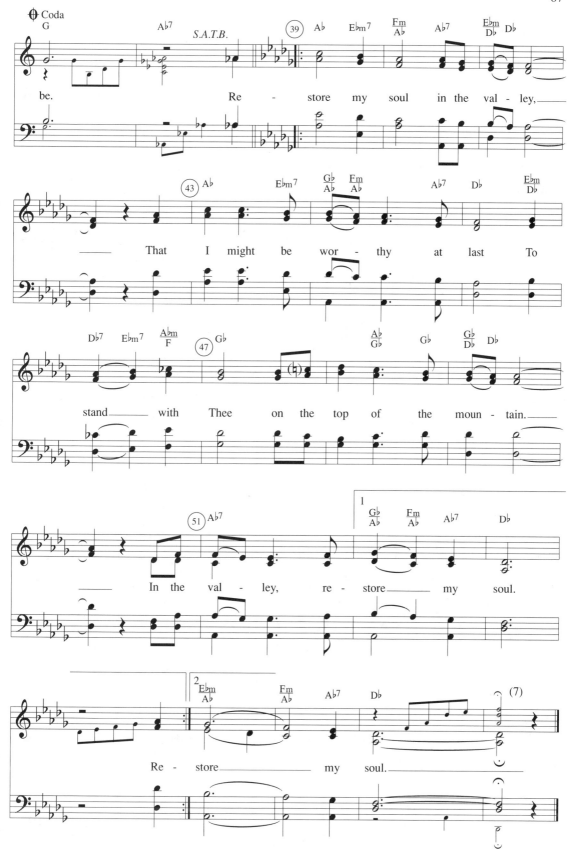

Yes, Lord, Yes

L. K.

LYNN KEESECKER
Arr. by Mosie Lister

I'll say yes, Lord,

yes! To Your will and to Your way. Yes, Lord,

yes! I will trust You and o-bey. When Your Spir-it speaks to me,

with my whole heart I'll a-gree And my an-swer will be

Not My Will, But Thine

H. C. B.

HUGH C. BENNER
Arr. by Mosie Lister

Jesus Is Coming Soon

R. E. W.

R. E. WINSETT
Arr. by Joseph Linn
and Mosie Lister

Holy Savior

M. L.

MOSIE LISTER

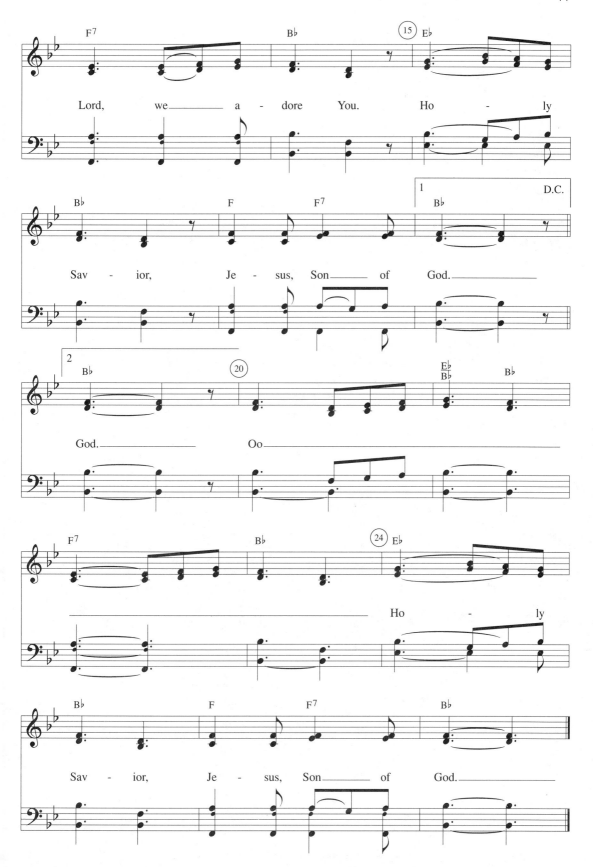

To God Be the Glory

FANNY J. CROSBY

WILLIAM H. DOANE
Arr. by Mosie Lister

He's Still the King of Kings

W. J. and GLORIA GAITHER

WILLIAM J. GAITHER
Arr. by Mosie Lister

Calvary's Love

G. N., P. M.

GREG NELSON and PHILL MCHUGH
Arr. by Mosie Lister

Our New Song of Praise

DAVID STEELE
Arr. by Mosie Lister

I Will Lift My Heart

D. E. W.

DAVID E. WILLIAMS
Arr. by Mosie Lister

The Light From Heaven

M. L.

MOSIE LISTER

With excitement ♩ = ca. 104

The Light from heav-en is shin-ing down on me.

I walk with Je-sus; I'm hap-py, glad, and free.

The Sun is shin-ing; the bet-ter way I see.

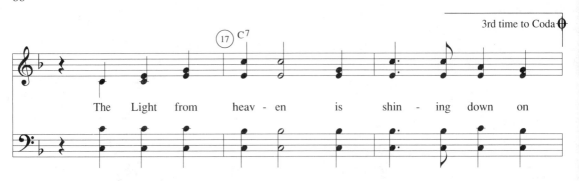

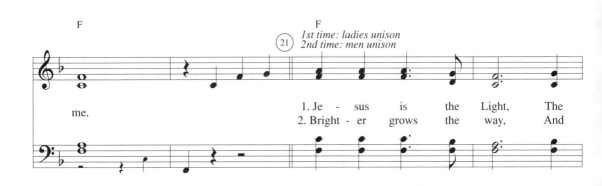

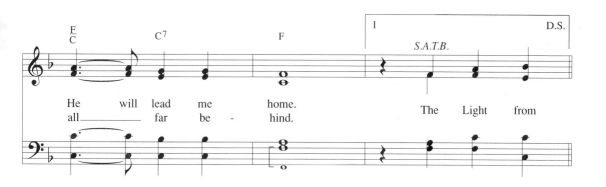

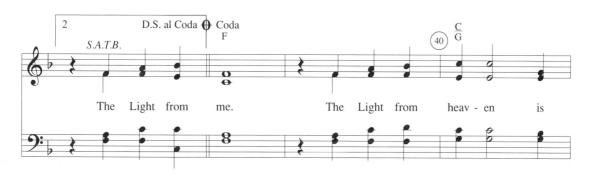

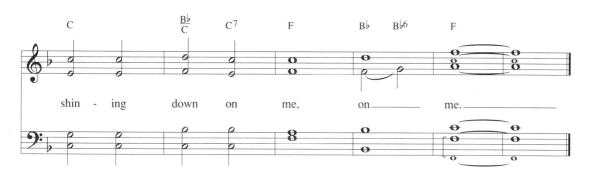

With God Nothing Is Impossible

D. H.

DOUG HOLCK
Arr. by Mosie Lister

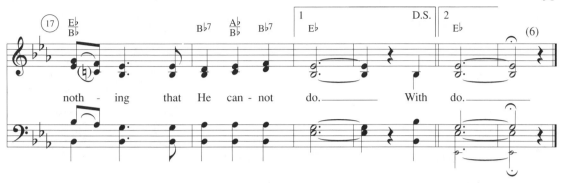

Right Now

O. S.

OTIS SKILLINGS
Arr. by Mosie Lister

I Can, I Will, I Do Believe

(*with* Take Me as I Am)

Trad. and ELIZA H. HAMILTON

Trad. and J. H. STOCKTON
Arr. by Lyndell Leatherman
and Mosie Lister

One of Your Children Needs You, Lord

M. L.

MOSIE LISTER

1st verse: Men sing melody, Ladies sing alto
2nd verse: ladies div., men "oo"

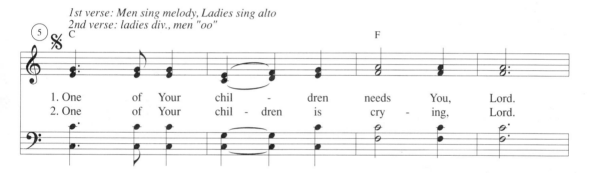

1. One of Your chil - dren needs You, Lord.
2. One of Your chil - dren is cry - ing, Lord.

One of Your chil - dren needs You, Lord. One of Your
One of Your chil - dren is cry - ing, Lord. One of Your

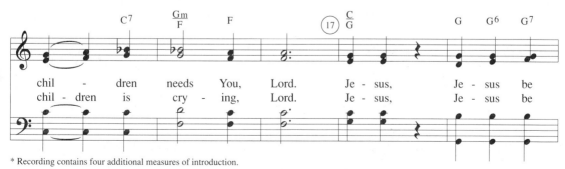

chil - dren needs You, Lord. Je - sus, Je - sus be
chil - dren is cry - ing, Lord. Je - sus, Je - sus be

Magnify Him

RANDY VADER and K. T.

KIRK TALLEY
Arr. by Mosie Lister

96

Love Through Me

M. L.

MOSIE LISTER

Prayerfully ♩ = ca. 72

1. Love through

me,   love through   me,   Oh,——   Lord,————————   love through
me,   weep through   me,   Oh,——   Lord,————————   weep through

me.   Some - where   some - bod - y   needs Your   love   to - day,   Oh,
me.   As—— long   as just   one   soul is   gone   a - stray,   Oh,

Lord,   love through   me.   2. Weep through
Lord,   weep through   me.   3. Speak through

99

Topical Index